SCHWARZENEGGER

AN UNAUTHORIZED BIOGRAPHY BY K. W. WOODS.

This publication is not authorized, endorsed, or licensed by Arnold Schwarzenegger,
Tri-Star, Carolco, or any affiliated companies.

PUBLICATIONS INTERNATIONAL, LTD.

Photo Credits:

AP/Wide World Photos, Inc.: Dennis Cook: 9 (top), 50 (bottom right); Columbia Pictures: 16; Dino Delaurentiis Corporation: Back Cover (center right), 22 (left); Gamma-Liaison: Michael Ginfray: 15 (left); David H. Kennerly: 32 (center); Barry King: 64; Sander: 4; D. Walker: 9 (bottom); Globe Photos, Inc.: 8, 12, 14 (right), 21, 22 (top), 35, 41, 45 (bottom), 46 (left); Arthur Gordon: 7; Bruce McBroom/Rangefinders: 54 (right), 55 (bottom), 56 (right); Michael Montfort: 6; Rangefinders: 44, 49, 53, 55; Zade Rosenthal/Rangefinders: 38 (right); IVE, Inc.: 44 (right); Yoram Kahana: 18, 19; London Features International: Greg DeGuire: 11 (left); Rodgers: 5; MCA: 23; Outline Press: Tony Costa: Back Cover (center); Photofest: Back Cover (top left), 14 (bottom), 15 (right), 20, 27, 33 (top); 38, 39, 45 (top), 47; Zade Rosenthal/Tri Star: 63; Shooting Star: 30-31, 32 (top), 33 (bottom); Carolco: 48; M. Montfort: Back Cover (bottom left); 25 (center, bottom); Zade Rosenthal: 36, 37; Norman Schreiber: Back Cover (bottom right); Donald Smetzer: 34; Universal: 56; 26; Sygma: Back Cover (center left), 28, 29, 42, 46 (right); Michael Childers: 24; Ruben Perez: 10; Trapper: 11 (right); T. Westenberger: 52; Tri-Star Pictures, Inc.: Carolco Home Video: Back Cover (top right), 50, 51; Aaron Rapaport/Carolco Pictures, Inc.: Front Cover, 3, 13; Zade Rosenthal: 58, 59, 60, 61, 62; Taft Entertainment Pictures/Keith Barish Productions: 40, 43; Twentieth Century Fox: 32; Universal City Studios Inc.: 22 (right), 54, 57.

CONTENTS

MUSCLEMAN
TO TERMINATOR

"In Austria, they say the country is known for its pastry, its music, and Arnold Schwarzenegger."

ARNOLD SCHWARZENEGGER

Above and opposite: The only things that Arnold Schwarzenegger needed to propel him from European obscurity to international fame were a will of steel, an unwavering desire to succeed, remarkable business savvy, and boundless self-confidence. Stir in a sense of humor and a solid grip on reality, and you have the ingredients that turned the unlikely name "Schwarzenegger" into a household word.

Arnold Schwarzenegger is the biggest movie star in the world. His face is familiar to people even in the most remote, isolated parts of the globe. His multimillion dollar salaries are the highest ever paid to a performer, and his movies are the biggest, most expensive, special-effects/action vehicles ever produced. Indeed, this 43-year-old native of Graz, Austria, has come a long way from his humble origins. Besides film stardom, his international fame encompasses a highly visible marriage to television newscaster Maria Shriver (and therefore entry into the Kennedy clan),

Schwarzenegger's success belies his quiet, ordinary origins. As a grade-school boy, he was just another pleasant-looking kid, but beneath that unassuming exterior was a star waiting to be born.

chumminess with American Presidents, and a growing business empire.

All this may seem like sheer luck, but if you ask the man himself, it was more the result of hard work, a relentless desire to succeed, and an incredibly strong sense of self-worth.

Arnold Schwarzenegger was born July 30, 1947, to a hausfrau mother and a police chief father who was once Europe's champion ice curler. Both parents instilled in him a sense of ambition. By the time he was 15, he was pumping iron, opting to become a bodybuilder.

"At first," he admitted, "it was just another competitive sport, a way of getting to the top. Then I realized it was actually an art form as well. I could change my body from one form to another. It was very close to sculpture."

Arnold considers his "healthy upbringing" a factor in his future success. "The only thing we didn't have was money," he recalled. "I had a lot of attention from my parents, a lot of love, and enough food—even though, growing up after the war was tough. . . ."

From the beginning, he knew what he wanted. For inspiration, he hung a picture of Reg Park, a former Mr. Universe, on his wall. "When I got into bodybuilding I said, 'This is it! I want to be Mr. Universe!' I always had a clear vision of what I wanted in front of me. . . . If you don't question whether you can make it, you're much more at ease. And you can't wait for the next push-up, the next workout, because you want to turn this vision into reality."

At 18, he was Mr. Europe Jr. and two years later he became the youngest Mr. Universe ever. "Arnold wouldn't be content with anything less than perfection," Maria Shiver told *Time*. Her

"When you're out there 10 years promoting something no one knew about and then you're responsible to put it on the map, you learn about promotion. Bodybuilding meant so much to me, I wanted everyone to know about it."
A.S.

From almost the beginning of his bodybuilding career, Arnold regarded the activity more as an art form than as a sport. He was excited by the thought of molding his physique to perfection. The result, as seen here, was good enough to win him an unprecedented number of titles in international competition.

Above: Success in bodybuilding turned Arnold into a public figure; autograph sessions became a routine event. **Top right:** Still, he cultivated a quieter side.

husband agrees: "I'm always hungry for more," he admitted. "I'm never satisfied. I was always very alive, hungry for doing things better than others. I'd set myself goals and then go after them with all my energy. Big goals."

After spending a year in the Austrian army, Arnold, whose last name means "black plowman," studied marketing for two years at the University of Munich. At the invitation of muscle entrepreneur Joe Weider, he came to the United States in 1968.

Coming to America was a natural extension of his self-image. "I always felt I had an American mentality," he explained. "I was born in the wrong country. When I came here, I was immediately sucked into the notion that everything was possible and that people were open-minded. I loved it. Americans don't start out with

negative attitudes as they do in Europe. People think big about achieving and making money and improving themselves. The whole idea of continuous progress."

That's precisely what the Austrian muscleman kept doing. Despite being staggered in 1972 by the deaths of his brother and father, Arnold persevered. Five times Mr. Universe and seven times Mr. Olympia, he started pondering his options for an all-out assault on a larger kind of fame, a higher level of success—through movies, mainly. He realized he had to market himself on the basis of his attributes, and he has done so very shrewdly. "When you have a unique look and a unique body like mine," he said, "you have to ask yourself, 'Is this a role that anybody else could play?' I don't want to fill in for Joe Blow."

Indeed, from an unimpressive debut in movies, Schwarzenegger has gone on to star in some of the most popular movies ever made—from the historical fantasy sagas *Conan the Barbarian* and *Conan the Destroyer* to the smashing sci-fi thrillers *The Terminator*, *Total Recall*, and *Terminator 2: Judgment Day*, to the mega-hit comedies *Twins* and *Kindergarten Cop*.

Arnold's strategy for success in movies had to do with a gradual "easing out into other areas." As he put it a couple of years ago, "I want to do different things, but not the opposite of what I've done, because that won't be justifiable from a business point of view. If you change everything abruptly, the audience won't go to see your movie. It's got to be gradual. Even in the beginning, I never said, 'Now I'm an actor, not a bodybuilder.' I didn't want to alienate my bodybuilding fans. It's the same with movies: if I inject some humor into my parts, at some point I could do a comedy. That's what I want to get into."

His game plan has worked and he has accomplished exactly what he set out to do, having surpassed in popularity and box-office grosses his main action-film competitor, Sylvester Stallone, and even Clint Eastwood, a man he admires. Not that Arnold has ever limited himself to acting. His business acumen has proved to be equally impressive. From his office in Santa Monica—he will soon move to bigger headquarters— he oversees a real estate empire, a mail order business, and various bodybuilding enterprises.

Arnold's triumph is particularly sweet because he achieved it in the face of ridicule and doubts from just about the entire movie industry—they laughed at his name, his accent, and his unusual looks. They're not laughing any more. In addition to his Hollywood success, Arnold has authored four best-selling books about bodybuilding, issues his own fitness videotapes, and lectures about sports before live audiences and on television. He gives his

"I have nothing to hide. I want people to get to know me and see my films, after they read about me."
A.S.

Above: Arnold meets with President George Bush after being named Chairman of the President's Council on Fitness. Left: Promoting fitness with <u>Saturday Night Live</u> star Kevin Nealen, half of the popular "Hans und Franz" team.

Arnold's 1986 marriage to television newscaster Maria Shriver paired him with a woman whose intelligence and ambition equals his own.

has been its national weight training coach for the past decade. In addition, he has been instrumental in implementing a prisoner rehab program through weight resistance training.

Known for his conservative politics, Arnold has been chummy with Presidents Reagan and Bush, but he insists that he just wants to make a contribution, make a positive impact on the system. He claims not to have ambition to run for office himself.

Much has been written about the irony of an arch Republican being married to an ultra-liberal. But Arnold and Maria know how to juggle differences of opinion, and have learned to agree to disagree. "I respect her point of view," Arnold asserted, "and she respects mine." They met in 1977 and were married nine years later. To date, they seem to have avoided conflicts that might have arisen because of their respective careers. "I'm an independent person," Arnold said, "independent enough to understand that Maria needs her own life and career and I'm very happy that she's goal-oriented and wants to accomplish a lot of things and be competitive out there."

His wife also helped him change his view about women. "When I left Europe," he laughed, "my ideal woman was the one who stayed at home and followed her husband. But I grew up and got re-educated here and understood the value of women

time and energy generously to young people in his capacity as Chairman of the President's Council on Fitness, insisting time and again that kids must be in good physical shape if they are to carve for themselves the lives they crave. He has also devoted time to the Special Olympics, and

doing their own thing." So much so, in fact, that he recently told *USA Today*, "At home, Maria is the Terminator!"

Although he has achieved almost everything one could aspire to, including a beautiful daughter named Katherine, Schwarzenegger refuses to become complacent—nor does he make the mistake of believing the Schwarzenegger hype that issues from movie-studio publicity departments. "Being the most muscular man in the world is funny," he admitted. "You have to be able to step back and look at yourself and then have a good laugh. Or the idea of being a great actor. That's a joke, too.

"I don't want to be taken overly seriously by anybody," he continued, "because I'm not a very serious person. I'm having fun making movies that entertain people. I don't sit there thinking about the craft of acting and getting traumatized. Why should I? My movies are hits and my books are best-sellers, but I don't feel 'successful.' Maybe people think, 'Is there something he can't do? He must think he's King Kong!' But that's not it. I struggle every day with my life and career, like everybody else."

Somehow, it's comforting to realize that this larger-than-life man, an "achiever" in every sense of the word, is not really a superman at all. He enjoys the fantasy, but lives the reality. He knows that life doesn't necessarily imitate the movies. Schwarzenegger has found success not through magic or happenstance, but through hard work and determination. In that, we can all take a measure of inspiration.

"What I liked about Maria was her healthy outlook on life in general—very smart, great sense of humor, driven, athletic. I have the ideal companion."
A.S.

With daughter Katherine (far left), and with Maria (left), accepting his star on Hollywood's Walk of Fame.

11

MUSCLEMAN TO MOVIE SUPERSTAR

"The key to all my movies is that good has to destroy evil."

ARNOLD SCHWARZENEGGER

Above: Sometimes, even world-class barbarians have to sit and wait. Arnold bides his time between setups during the shoot of **Conan the Barbarian,** the hit movie that was the first important step on his climb to film stardom. **Opposite:** Decked out in full leather in his mega-hit thriller, **Terminator 2: Judgment Day.** At one time a bodybuilder who dabbled in acting, Schwarzenegger needed barely more than a decade to transform himself into a superstar actor who happens to be a bodybuilder. He is today the world's #1 box-office attraction.

With the "performance" aspect of bodybuilding a key part of the sport, it was inevitable that Arnold Schwarzenegger would seek and find new arenas in which to exhibit his ample physical attributes. Movies were an obvious choice, and the industry gave him his first chance soon after he crossed the Atlantic. Brimming with muscular enthusiasm and youthful energy, and helped by his bodybuilding guru, Joe Weider, Arnold landed the lead in director Arthur Seidelman's low-budget 1970 movie, *Hercules in New York* (also known as *Hercules–the Movie* and *Hercules Goes Bananas*). Billed as "Arnold Strong," the largely unknown Schwarzenegger co-starred with skinny comic actor Arnold Stang. Although the casting of the bodybuilder as the mythological hero made sense even then, unleashing the character on modern-day Manhattan certainly didn't. And the fact that an unaccented voice was dubbed over his own added little flavor to this odd, noticeably unfunny film.

After this unpromising debut, Arnold waited six years before his next movie break: a featured role in director Bob Rafelson's *Stay Hungry,* an eccentric, serio-comic tale about bodybuilders in the "New South." Six years is a long time between movie projects, and it seemed as though Arnold had lost interest in acting altogether. "I only fell into acting by accident," he told *US* magazine. "Bob Rafelson needed a muscular actor and he couldn't find one. The slim look was the thing then, so he gave bodybuilders screen tests and I got the job."

Arnold played Joe Santo, an intelligent bodybuilder and Mr. Universe contestant, who fascinates Craig (Jeff Bridges), a scion of a privileged family who tries to establish his own identity while romancing a receptionist (Sally Field). Based on Charles

Above: Arnold made his film debut in a low-budget obscurity called Hercules in New York. **Right and above right:** He had a much better showcase in Stay Hungry, which featured Sally Field.

Gaines's novel, the movie won serious although mostly negative reviews. Critics considered it confused and disjointed, but they had only kind words for Arnold. The role gave him an opportunity to lift weights in a Batman getup, and voice the philosophical advice that gives the picture its title. "I don't believe in getting too comfortable," he tells Craig. "Stay hungry."

Frank Rich, writing in the *New York Post*, praised Arnold's "sweet non-macho, heterosexual appeal," but Vincent Canby of *The New York Times* had favorable words for the actor only as long as he kept his clothes on, but not when he revealed his "huge, grotesquely muscled body."

Despite its critical and commercial failure, *Stay Hungry* was a legitimate studio film and a respectable credit for Arnold. But a year later, in 1977, it was *Pumping Iron*, another movie based on a book by Charles Gaines, that brought the neophyte actor wide attention. This documentary about body building, which also starred Lou Ferrigno (who later found fame as TV's *The Incredible Hulk*), not only helped legitimize a sport and a subculture that were previously hardly taken seriously, but revealed the 29-year-old Schwarzenegger's screen appeal, heavy accent and all. Critic Richard Schickel wrote in *Time*, "A cool, shrewd and boyish charmer, [Schwarzenegger] exudes the easy confidence of a man who has always known he

"I'd do anything I think could be a successful movie and could be fun to do. That's really the bottom line."
A.S.

Left and above: Arnold shows his stuff to a group of genteel ladies in <u>Pumping Iron</u>.

will be a star of some kind."

And the experience certainly whetted the actor's appetite for the movies. "Bodybuilding has a lot to do with acting," Arnold said in publicity material released in conjunction with *Pumping Iron*. "When you're competing, you're showing off your talent. Your attitude in front of an audience or before the judges is much the same as working before the camera."

Directed by George Butler, the movie itself was regarded as intelligent, charming, and well-made, while allowing a glimpse into Arnold's real self: In one scene, he compares bodybuilding to the pleasures of sex, and admits that he skipped his father's funeral so that he would not miss a training session.

Arnold followed *Pumping Iron* with *The Villain*, a cartoonish

Even Arnold's most devoted fans agree that The Villain simply does not work: not as a western, and certainly not as a comedy. But at least Arnold looked good in the cowboy outfit.

1979 comedy western directed by stunt-oriented Hal Needham. The picture was a disaster. Arnold played "Handsome Stranger," a dumb, virile cowboy who's also the good guy; Kirk Douglas was cast as roguish outlaw "Cactus Jack," and Ann-Margret played the lusty "Charming Jones." As for Arnold, his newly discovered screen charm seemed to have gone into remission. *Variety* declared that "Schwarzenegger shows little development as an actor since *Stay Hungry*," while Janet Maslin in *The New York Times* termed him "a weight on the movie." *Newsweek*'s David Ansen described his range of expressions as "considerably more limited than the horse's."

In all fairness, the movie's flaws go far beyond Arnold's contribution. He simply made a bad choice—which didn't stop him from repeating the mistake by agreeing to do a cameo the same year in *Scavenger Hunt*, a frantic comedy about a mad rush for an inheritance. Arnold played an overzealous gym instructor named Lars in this unfunny farce that co-starred Ruth Gordon and Richard Benjamin. Director Michael Schultz apparently thought he was going to top *It's a Mad Mad Mad Mad World*, but he was mistaken.

Schwarzenegger's screen career had shifted into low gear, but he was at least able to show his stuff before a large audience with his next assignment, *The Jayne Mansfield Story*, a TV-movie that

"I was convinced I could make millions of dollars in acting. People told me, 'Arnold, with a strange accent, a strange body, and a strange name, you won't make it in this profession.' But I saw it."
A.S.

Arnold played Hungarian bodybuilder Mickey Hargitay in <u>The Jayne Mansfield Story</u>. He handled the part well, but was really just window dressing for star Loni Anderson.

was telecast in 1980. Loni Anderson starred as the Hollywood blonde bombshell of the 1950s, portraying her as a sensitive woman who yearned for love and artistic fulfillment. Arnold was suitably cast as Jayne's husband, Hungarian bodybuilder Mickey Hargitay. While the movie offered no surprises, it did provide Arnold with his first TV credit, and some not-bad reviews. Although John J. O'Connor of *The New York Times* panned the film, he made a point of mentioning Arnold's "nice, unaffected gentleness." It was a nice compliment, but gentleness was not the quality that was to become Schwarzenegger's stock in trade.

CONAN THE BARBARIAN

(1982)

Universal

With

Arnold Schwarzenegger,

James Earl Jones,

Max von Sydow,

Sandahl Bergman,

William Smith,

Gerry Lopez.

Directed by John Milius.

Written by Milius and Oliver Stone.

129 minutes.

Set in the mythical Hyborian Age, a grim period in the world's pre-history, *Conan the Barbarian* is a fantasy-adventure focusing on a man described as "thief, reiver, slayer with gigantic melancholies and gigantic mirth." Cimmerian by birth, Conan (Arnold) had been captured as a child by Thulsa Doom (James Earl Jones), head of the snake cult of Set and leader of the raiding Vanir; Conan's parents were savagely murdered by the Vanir. After fifteen years of agonizing slavery—including periods chained to the Wheel of Pain to grind grain, and messy work as a Pit Fighter—Conan emerges as a man of formidable physique and an indomitable spirit.

Freed one day by his owner, Conan joins forces with Subotai the Mongol (Gerry Lopez) and Valeria, Queen of Thieves (Sandahl Bergman). They resolve to kill the vicious Thulsa Doom, and seek the solution to "the riddle of steel," rumored to confer the ultimate power. The three embark on hair-raising adventures that climax with the rescue of the king's daughter.

Conan the Barbarian was the first sword and sorcery picture to be released by a major studio in a long time, and it clicked with audiences right away, mostly because of the images of the very muscular Arnold fighting a 40-foot snake, making love to a witch who turns into a whirlwind, and engaging in breathtaking sword fights. These visual feasts had been absent from the screen since the early-1960s heyday of Steve Reeves, who also had muscles, but nothing to match the Schwarzenegger charisma.

Created in the 1930s by pulp-magazine writer Robert E. Howard, Conan found success as a Marvel Comics character in the seventies, and then as a screen hero via Schwarzenegger. **At right,** Conan dallies with Valeria (Sandahl Bergman). **Opposite:** Conan is crucified in what is probably the most memorable scene of Conan the Barbarian.

The $20 million movie, based on the hero created during the 1930s by pulp-magazine writer Robert E. Howard, was shot in Spain. For heightened realism, Schwarzenegger, Bergman (a trained dancer), and Lopez (a surfer) performed nearly all of their own stunts. Arnold endured some pain during the production: He tore a ligament in a fall from his horse; had the back of his head bitten by camel; and fell

Robert E. Howard conceived Conan as a man of violent action. Fittingly, then, both of the Conan films bristle with energy—and the sharp edge of steel.

down a 20-foot rock on his back. But he remained unfazed. "[Director] John Milius promised us dirt and pain, and there's been a lot of both—as well as fun," Arnold laughed at the time. And he was amply rewarded. The movie, which grossed over $50 million, established him as an action hero to be reckoned with.

"The picture is a winner because Conan is a winner,"

Arnold told the *New York Post.* "Conan is an honorable man. His life is based on strength: of body, mind, and spirit. He's the kind of person an audience can identify with. He never gives up." No doubt about that, for, as moviegoers discovered, Conan is the sort of man who can bite off the head of a marauding vulture while tied to a cross!

"Conan doesn't think—he just acts," Schwarzenegger added. "No ones gives him a break. He has to do everything himself." Schwarzenegger told *Pulse* magazine, "I understood the character. He got strong through adversity. I was meant to play the part. . . . [Even] my accent was an asset in *Conan,* because I was supposed to be from a different era, so they wanted me to talk differently from everyone else."

Not everyone cheered the movie. Some critics lamented its excessive gore and violence. Others sneered at its pretentiousness and macho philosophy, a trademark of director Milius. Still others saw it as heavy-handed and compared the epic unfavorably with the more humorous *Star Wars* and *Raiders of the Lost Ark.* One critic termed Arnold "silly" and Vincent Canby of *The New York Times,* who described *Conan* as "the archetypal escapist film . . . a kiddie fantasy for grown-ups," described Arnold as "the male equivalent of the late Jayne Mansfield," and complained that he lacked grace. "He often looks as if he hadn't done his warm-up exercises properly," Canby quipped.

Criticism of this sort apparently didn't hurt the picture's box-office performance, and didn't bother the star too much, either. Discussing the film's violence with *Pulse*, Schwarzenegger remarked, "Face it, this is not a movie about babysitters. It's about a barbarian!"

Everyone's favorite Cimmerian swordsman was back in *Conan the Destroyer*. In this frantic action-adventure, Conan undertakes a quest for a magical key, guarded by a wizard (Mako), which will unlock a vast treasure of mysterious significance. Conan sets off on behalf of the wicked Queen Taramis (Sarah Douglas), who wants her niece, Princess Jehnna (Olivia D'Abo) to be the treasure's beneficiary. In return, the queen will use her magic powers to bring Valeria, Conan's dead love, back to life. The expedition includes the virgin princess; Malak (Tracey Walter), a comic sidekick who's none too eager to confront danger; Bombaata (Wilt Chamberlain), the queen's hired assassin; and Zula (Grace Jones), a scantily clad female warrior who becomes Conan's ally. The group faces a number of dangers, topped off by Conan's climactic battle with a hideous monster (designed by E.T. creator Carlo Rambaldi).

For this sequel to *Conan the Barbarian*, Arnold was called upon to display a stronger sense of humor than before, and an extra measure of charm—facets of his personality that had not been necessary in the saga's previous chapter. Director Richard Fleischer, who termed his star "the biggest and the best," opted for less gore and more physical action than in the original movie. Surprisingly, he wanted his star to display an even bigger physique than in the first film. Arnold recalled that "Fleischer pulled me aside and said, 'This is a little difficult to say, but could you put on more muscles?'" The actor laughed. "It was quite a shock to me, but it motivated me tremendously." Arnold went on to add 10 pounds, working out five hours a day for a full two months prior to the shoot. And it worked.

"People today want to see the hero look heroic," Arnold told *Marquee*, "not just act heroically. And I'm not against macho. I'm not against being a man. Americans went through a period where it was a bit negative to say you were rugged, macho. I never felt like that."

Still, the actor stressed Conan's vulnerability as an integral part of his portrayal. "If somebody would've asked me to play Hercules," he said, "I wouldn't have done it. Anyone who can push columns apart—you can't sympathize with a guy like that in a fight. Anyone who wipes out a temple, how can he have any trouble? But Conan is a human being: he's vulnerable, he's fallen in love, and mourns his beloved's death. And you get caught up in

CONAN THE DESTROYER
(1984)
Universal
With
Arnold Schwarzenegger,
Grace Jones,
Wilt Chamberlain,
Mako,
Tracey Walter,
Olivia D'Abo,
Sarah Douglas.
Directed by Richard Fleischer.
Written by Stanley Mann.
103 minutes.

Arnold is touched up by a makeup artist between scenes on the set of Conan the Destroyer.

"I never had any difficulty with my leading ladies—as long as I stayed far enough from Grace Jones. She was hitting everybody with a stick over the head! She's wild. Fantastic. We admired each other right away, and she's become a good pal of mine."

A.S.

his fight scenes because they really are life and death."

Although the sequel didn't win better reviews than its predecessor, and grossed a more modest but still respectable $30 million, Arnold's reputation as a box office draw became further solidified. At the very least,

Schwarzenegger was aware that he had grown considerably as a screen actor. Discussing his first appearance as Conan with the *Cable Guide*, he remarked, "I didn't fully rely on my acting. [Now] I had to make the next step and rely less on the body and more on the acting."

Right and above: Singer Grace Jones—an imposing physical presence in her own right—was well cast opposite Arnold in Conan the Destroyer. **Far right and opposite:** Schwarzenegger makes it clear for all to see why he was the embodiment of Conan.

THE TERMINATOR
(1984)
Orion
With
Arnold Schwarzenegger,
Michael Biehn,
Linda Hamilton,
Lance Henriksen,
Paul Winfield,
Rick Rossovich.
Directed by James Cameron.
Written by Cameron and Gale Ann Hurd.
108 minutes.

As the Cyberdyne Systems Terminator Model 101 in the original film, Arnold made a formidable impression on moviegoers. His famous line, "I'll be back," has since become a classic.

Schwarzenegger tackled the title role in *The Terminator*, which electrified audiences in 1984. A cybrog (a robot with the form of a man), the Terminator has been sent from the year 2029 to present-day Los Angeles. Representing a world that has become dominated by machines, the cyborg has been programmed to seek out and kill a young waitress named Sarah Connor (Linda Hamilton) before she can conceive the son who will lead the future-era humans to victory over their mechanical enemies. At the same time, Kyle Reese (Michael Biehn), a young but tough guerilla fighter, is also sent back in time to protect the unsuspecting Sarah from the relentless "killing machine" on her trail. Against all odds, Reese is determined to "terminate" the Terminator before it can fulfill its mission.

As the terrified Sarah dodges the Terminator and Kyle pursues him in a deadly game of search and destroy, the cyborg crushes anything—and anyone— that stumbles into its path. Against a murderous force of such magnitude, the police, including inspector Traxler (Paul Winfield) and his assistant, Vukovich (Lance Henriksen), stand little chance of making an impact. "I'll be back," the cyborg tells a police sergeant before crashing into the station and riddling everyone in it with bullets. But humanity triumphs during the film's thrilling climax, when the Terminator ends up in the clutches of a hydraulic press.

The Terminator marks the real turning point in Schwarzenegger's career. "It has radically changed the Hollywood community's opinion of me," the star told *USA Today*. "This movie has legitimized me as an actor." The picture won almost unanimous raves from critics, mostly for James Cameron's dazzling direction and Stan Winston's eye-popping special effects. Critics respectfully noted the picture's B-movie elements and futuristic *film noir* style—Variety termed the film "a cross between *The Road Warrior* and *Blade Runner*" —yet remarked that the filmmaker managed to transcend genre clichés and create an original work. One legitimate gripe was voiced by author/TV writer Harlan Ellison, who claimed that the film's script was suspiciously similar to the "Demon with a Glass Hand" episode of *The Outer Limits* that he had written some 20 years before; cable-TV and video prints of *The Terminator* give Ellison a special credit line.

Audiences cheered mightily for the picture, which could have doubled its respectable $30 million gross if the distributor had marketed it more imaginatively. Arnold explained, "Orion did a publicity campaign totally directed at the youth male audience, and what happened was that just as many women came to see it. They liked the look of the leather jacket, the short hair and the sunglasses—the punk touch."

"When you're playing a robot, you can get away much more doing evil things than if you play a regular human being."
A.S.

Costuming and lighting in <u>The Terminator</u> helped convey the idea that Arnold's character is a threat to mankind. **Top:** The bar-like shadows across Arnold's face, a technique borrowed from <u>film noir</u>, carry a warning of potential danger. **Middle:** His costume, consisting of a leather jacket and heavy boots, is reminiscent of the garb worn by motorcycle gangs. **Bottom:** The Terminator's punk haircut and dark sunglasses help suggest a futuristic killer, whose fashionably cool attire is attractive yet sinister.

Much of the appeal of *The Terminator* lies in the surprise of seeing Arnold for the first time as the villain, a break from the larger-than-life but essentially gentle-giant screen persona he'd been associated with. Although he was initially offered a chance to play Reese, the story's human hero, Arnold refused to portray just another nice guy and opted instead for the murderous cyborg,

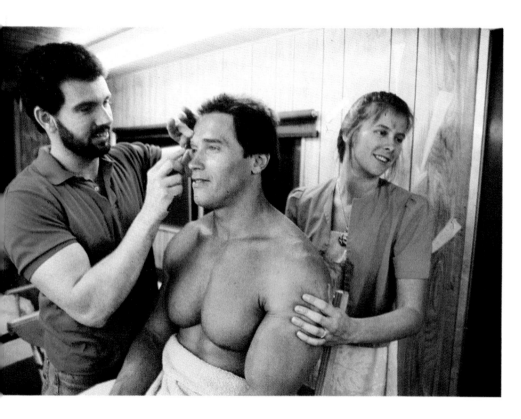

Arnold sits completely still while makeup experts apply the steel-like plate that represents part of the cyborg's skeletal infrastructure. The film's use of special effects and makeup were minimal yet so effective that reviewers often raved about them.

which necessitated a rewrite of the part since the killing machine had originally been conceived as faceless and without character.

Although Schwarzenegger spent most of his screen time dressed in a state of the art leather outfit, fans of his memorable physique got a chance to see him in the raw, in the scene in which the cyborg first arrives in present-day L.A. Still,

as he told *Interview* magazine, "*Terminator* made people think, 'Yes, let's get Arnold to be a regular action hero—with clothes.' It was understood that I had the body, but I didn't have to show it to make a point."

The Terminator himself never says more than a few words at a time, and his emotional range is close to zero, but the movie ends up being humorous precisely because of the cyborg's unrelenting grimness. Very carefully written one-liners and clever responses (for a robot) also endeared him to audiences.

"I like the Terminator," Schwarzenegger said. "I'd like to be as resolved as he was and have that kind of power and do the things he's able to do—an indestructible creature." Arnold knew that he "wanted to play the part of the Terminator as soon as I started reading the script. And getting the chance to play that kind of character has really helped me as an actor." And as he revealed to a reporter from *People*, "It's more challenging to play a robot than a human." The role also required him to be ultra-patient as he sat for long hours while all the special make-up was applied.

The film was made in and around Los Angeles on a shoestring budget of $6 million, which makes its visual accomplishments all the more striking. Much of the effects work was done with cleverly designed miniature props and sets that were seamlessly integrated

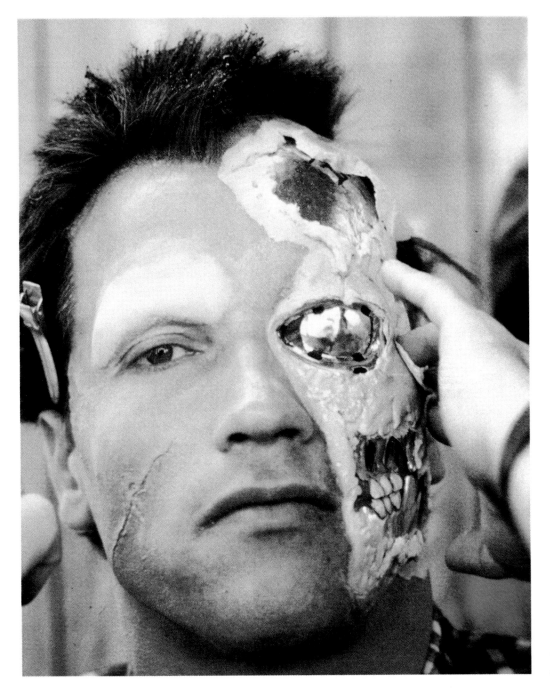

"A lot of guys would like to destroy a police station. Even the police guys came to me in the gym and said, 'That was my favorite scene!'"
A.S.

The most frightening aspect about Arnold's Terminator was that he proved to be virtually unstoppable. After having his eye ripped from its socket, he performs cyborg surgery on himself to restore his vision. In the film's relentless climax, he is shot, mutilated, and dragged by moving vehicles. He survives a fiery crash, which burns the human flesh from his "endoskeleton," to pursue Sarah Connor to the film's unforgettable conclusion.

into the live-action footage. Key moments of the Terminator's final, skeletal rampage were filmed in stop-motion animation, an effective but low-tech process that utilizes small, jointed puppets that are filmed one frame at a time. In all, *The Terminator* proved to be a special-effects feast.

Following the immediate success of the movie, writer-director James Cameron acknowledged the possibility of a sequel—never mind that the Terminator buys the farm at the movie's climax. "He's a machine," Cameron told *The New York Times,* "and machines are mass-produced, so there might be another one in the warehouse. . . ."

RED SONJA
(1985)
MGM/UA
With
Arnold Schwarzenegger,
Brigitte Nielsen,
Sandahl Bergman,
Paul Smith,
Ernie Reyes Jr.,
Ronald Lacey.
Directed by Richard Fleischer.
Written by Clive Exton and George
MacDonald Fraser.
89 minutes.

Red Sonja chronicles the lusty adventures of the title heroine (Brigitte Nielsen), who leads a peaceful life on a farm before the army of the evil Queen Gedren (Sandahl Bergman), accompanied by her cruel henchmen, Ikol (Ronald Lacey), murders her family and rapes her. Red Sonja—named for the color of her hair— vows vengeance and is granted extraordinary powers by a mysterious vision on the condition that she not give herself to a man until he defeats her in a fair fight.

Sonja sets off on her solitary quest in a land of strange beasts and cruel people, learning that Gedren has stolen a sacred talisman that may impart total power. Sonja decides to destroy both the talisman and its new owner, the scar-faced queen, to save the planet from destruction.

To do so, she reluctantly joins forces with the arrogant Prince Tarn (Ernie Reyes, Jr.) and his bumbling protector, Falkon (Paul Smith), yet refuses the help of Kalidor (Arnold), a mysterious stranger with a unique mastery of the sword. But Sonja reconsiders her position when Kalidor proves to be more than a match for her.

Red Sonja reunited Arnold with the source material of pulp writer Robert E. Howard, director Richard Fleischer, and *Conan the Barbarian* co-star Sandahl Bergman. Unfortunately, the result was decidedly lackluster; *USA Today* critic Mike Clark called *Red Sonja* "a strong sleeping pill." Perhaps because of responses like that one, this sword and sorcery epic was to be Arnold's last foray into the genre. Although it was a resounding box office flop (a

Child actor Ernie Reyes, Jr., a kung fu expert, co-starred as the haughty Prince Tarn. Reyes went on to greater glory as Keno in Teenage Mutant Ninja Turtles II: The Secret of the Ooze.

special disappointment after the success of *The Terminator*), *Red Sonja* didn't prove a setback to Schwarzenegger's career. Instead, it inspired him to be more selective in his choice of vehicles.

Red Sonja, which was filmed in Italy, wasn't conceived as an Arnold vehicle at all. "[Producer] Dino De Laurentiis said he wanted me to do a cameo,"

recalled the star, "and have me work for three weeks—and then he went and sold the picture with my name above the title—and that's bad news. I told him it was a big mistake. It didn't work—you can't fool people."

Although Arnold does have some spectacular action scenes—notably his wrestling match with the Killing Machine, a mechanical creature resembling a crocodile—the film as a whole is disappointingly flat. Essentially, the movie tells the heroine's story. Newcomer Brigitte Nielsen (who later did a brief stint as

Mrs. Sylvester Stallone) lacked the acting skills to impress audiences. Worse, the paying customers felt cheated because the person they had paid to see in the first place was Arnold. The star learned quickly that to play second banana was simply not his forte.

"I'm not interested in violence, but I'm not against macho, either."
A.S.

Top: Brigitte Nielsen and Arnold did not have the chemistry that he and Sandahl Bergman had in <u>Conan the Barbarian</u>. **Above left:** Chemistry aside, the pair did make a handsome couple. **Above:** Sonja fights Kalidor, who defeats the red-headed beauty in battle but wins her heart.

COMMANDO
(1985)
20th Century-Fox
With
Arnold Schwarzenegger,
Rae Dawn Chong,
Dan Hedaya,
Vernon Wells,
James Olson,
David Patrick Kelly,
Alyssa Milano.
Directed by Mark L. Lester.
Written by Steven E. DeSouza.
88 minutes.

Alyssa Milano gets a boost from Arnold during a scene from Commando, an action-packed adventure that outgrossed The Terminator. Soon after acting in this film, young Alyssa landed the role of Samantha, the adolescent daughter, in the ABC sitcom Who's the Boss?

Commando is the story of Colonel John Matrix (Arnold), a peerless commando and former leader of a special operations task force specializing in political hot spots. Matrix, no longer considered useful by his superiors and forced into retirement, lives under a new identity in a rural haven with his 11-year-old daughter Jenny (Alyssa Milano). Suddenly, he must confront his tumultuous past when a Latin American dictator he helped depose, General Arius (Dan Hedaya), works with one of Matrix's former men, Bennett (Vernon Wells), to track him down and kidnap his daughter. Arius's plan is to regain power in his nation by killing the current president-elect.

Although Matrix soon finds himself under fire in a no-win situation, a stewardess (Rae Dawn Chong) he abducts during a getaway at an airport reluctantly agrees to help. Together, they run into more than they had bargained for: On an island off the coast of California, the dictator has gathered a large force of men that includes Bennett, the renegade agent who wants to prove himself superior to his former boss; and Sully (David Patrick Kelly), an evil punk. Besides the stewardess, Matrix's only other ally is General Franklin Kirby (James Olson), the man who trained him and gave him a new identity. Trouble is that Kirby is always one step behind the action.

Regardless of the odds, Matrix

becomes a murderous vengeance machine as he sets out to terminate the kidnappers. Following a climactic assault on their island refuge and the destruction of Bennett and the other culprits, Matrix is reunited with his daughter.

Commando is a violent fantasy that garnered a cool critical response, and not without some justification. *USA Today* critic Jack Curry pointed out, for example, that the hero massacres

"When I deal with a studio, I make what I want clear right at the beginning. I muscle my way through it. But as soon as we get to the set, I step back and let the director have his space."
A.S.

The relentless action scenes and violent encounters in <u>Commando</u> left some reviewers cold. One writer took the time to tally up the actual body count. Supposedly, 92 characters were machine-gunned, thrown off cliffs, knifed, pitchforked, axed, pummelled, and just plain shot within the 88-minute running time.

innocent bystanders as well as the bad guys, a behavior flaw that reduces Matrix's moral authority. But moviegoers were apparently not bothered by such quibbles, and responded warmly to the picture. An undeniable part of the film's appeal is Arnold's byplay with Rae Dawn Chong, who was a marvelous, wisecracking sidekick, and an effective counterbalance to the film's violence. "Matrix has 11 hours to save his daughter's life,"

Arnold commented, "so he can't have too much fun. That would be unacceptable." It's for this reason that Chong got the opportunity to serve as comic relief.

Not that the iron man himself doesn't crack a joke from time to time. After telling one villain that he likes him and will kill him last, he drops him off a precipice and shouts after him, "I lied." Later, when asked what he has done with the man, Matrix

"In movies like <u>Commando</u>, what stands out is my presence. I dominated, and people went to see them because of me."
A.S.

responds, "I let him go." Similarly, an invitation from Bennett to duel to the death with knives is accepted thusly: "Let's party!"

Commando outgrossed *The Terminator* by a small amount, confirming Arnold as a genuine crowd pleaser, and a box-office force. But the star himself contends that the importance of the movie for his career has to do with the new image he projected in it.

"In the beginning of the film," he said, "I play a loving, gentle and understanding father . . . I educate and protect my daughter. I show a human, sensitive side that I never have a chance to show. I can play that. The movie was well written and it showed a soldier in combat, but also in his private life, which rarely happens."

Commando required Schwarzenegger to perfect his fighting skills, an accomplishment that didn't escape the critics. D.J.R. Bruckner of *The New York Times* commended Arnold for his mastery of fencing, karate,

Top: Costar Rae Dawn Chong added some much-needed comic relief to the grim action of the film. **Above:** The real Arnold grins among a display of film posters, which offer an image of the muscleman more familiar to his fans. **Right:** The use of the Steadicam to film Arnold in some of the action scenes made viewers feel as though they were fighting alongside him.

and knife-fighting, and praised him for being "more supple and faster in *Commando* than he has ever been." Even fight choreographer Mike Vendrell was impressed. "I was told bodybuilders were slow," he said, "but Arnold moved like a cat!"

The star himself acknowledges the physical danger in doing his own stunts, a long-time tradition in his film career. "I was injured, but it was never more than a few days' layoff," he recalled. In the scene where Matrix exits a plane during takeoff, Arnold had to "climb down the wheel but there was no place to step on—if I made a mistake, I would have been crushed by the wheel. The danger was real! But sometimes the emotional strain and the psychological pressure you go through almost equal the physical pain and danger."

"There's nobody else but Arnold who could have done

what he did," said director Mark Lester. Co-star Rae Dawn Chong enthused, "Arnold is so beautiful inside and out! We were having so much fun on the set, but when it was time to work, we just did. He's very generous and gentle. And a real movie star."

"I can now read scripts and decide which one I want to do and then set it up with the studio. It's a comfortable position but, like everything else, it's a double-edged sword."

A.S.; Boston Globe

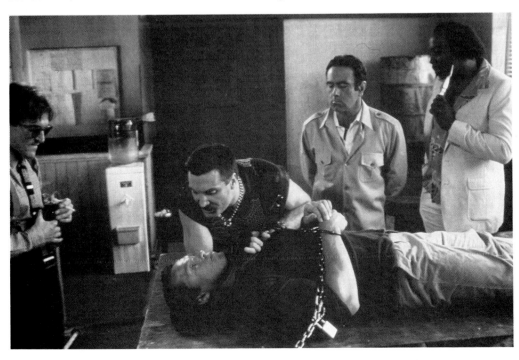

Top: Arnold—as John Matrix, the father-turned-commando—trashes a helicopter with a multi-barrelled rocket launcher. Left: Bennett, played by veteran character actor Vernon Wells, taunts Matrix as he lies chained and helpless.

RAW DEAL
(1986)
De Laurentiis Entertainment
With
Arnold Schwarzenegger,
Kathryn Harrold,
Darren McGavin,
Sam Wanamaker,
Paul Shenar,
Robert Davi,
Steven Hill,
Joe Regalbuto.
Directed by John Irvin.
Written by Gary M. DeVore and Norman
Wexler.
97 minutes.

Above: The love scenes Arnold played in Raw Deal with beautiful Kathryn Harrold were a new sort of challenge for the action-oriented star. **Opposite:** In general, the film provided Arnold's fans with plenty of macho action.

In *Raw Deal*, ex-FBI agent Mark Kaminsky (Arnold), forced to retire for excessive brutality, is offered a chance to reinstate himself if he manages to infiltrate the Chicago mob, headed by Luigi Patrovita (Sam Wanamaker), and destroy it from the inside. He is recruited by Shannon (Darren McGavin), who also wants to uncover the FBI "mole" who is collaborating with the mob.

After faking his death in an oil refinery explosion, Kaminsky assumes a new identity—that of Joseph Brenner—and destroys a gambling outfit headed by Patrovita's rival (Steven Hill). Over the objection of a Patrovita enforcer named Max (Robert Davi), Brenner is rewarded with a job by Patrovita's second in command, Paulo Rocca (Paul Shenar). Max hires Monique (Kathryn Harrold), a pretty, in-debt gambler to seduce Brenner and discover his real game. But Brenner uses the attempted seduction to further prove his "loyalty." Still, Max does find out that Brenner isn't the man he pretends to be and involves him in a "hit," where he's required to assassinate Shannon. In the ensuing scuffle, Shannon is killed by Max, who, in turn, is eliminated by our hero. Then Brenner singlehandedly finishes off Patrovita and his entire gang.

Raw Deal was not Arnold's first foray into the gangster genre. "It's contemporary," the star told *The San Francisco Chronicle*, "but still hard-boiled, and I wear three piece suits and double-breasted jackets, with my hair slicked back. . . ."

A modified appearance was only part of Arnold's approach to the role. He remarked to the *Chronicle* that John Irvin, whom he terms "an actor's director," "works on your neuroses, trying to get the most out of you. I must say, I like that. Acting is like body building: the more you do it, the better you get—and each time I see myself getting closer to the perfect delivery of the scene."

Arnold also enjoyed the tame screen romance with Harrold, whose character must labor to seduce him. "We don't get into the sex right away," he explained to the *Chronicle*. "That's old stuff. Instead, we have a relationship that keeps growing."

Gangster thrillers have been a staple of Hollywood filmmaking since the early days of movies. *Raw Deal* is slick, but familiar. High on carnage, the movie didn't make much of a splash with either critics or moviegoers, and was Schwarzenegger's first box-office flop since *Red Sonja*. But at least *The New York Times*' Vincent Canby, by no means a Schwarzenegger fan, wrote, "The former Mr. Universe wears well as a film personality, partly because there's something comic about the massiveness of his frame and the gentleness of his manners (when in repose)."

Not a bad assessment for a film that was far from a high point of Arnold's screen career.

PREDATOR
(1987)
20th Century-Fox
With
Arnold Schwarzenegger,
Carl Weathers,
Elpidia Carrillo,
Bill Duke,
Jesse Ventura,
Sonny Landham,
Kevin Peter Hall.
Directed by John McTiernan.
Written by Jim Thomas & John Thomas.
107 minutes.

Predator opens with Major Dutch Schaefer (Arnold) going on what seems to be a routine mission as leader of a military rescue unit. The group's goal? To locate men kidnapped by a band of terrorists and held captive in the South American jungle. Schaefer is tough, and the men in his unit are formidable in their own right. There's Dillon (Carl Weathers), Schaefer's old combat buddy who has become a CIA operative; Mac (Bill Duke), whose sanity hangs by a fragile thread; the tobacco-chewing Blain (Jesse Ventura); and Billy (Sonny Landham), an Indian tracker. When the unit spots and destroys a guerilla camp, it becomes clear that the men they hoped to save have already been executed, and in a most horrible manner: They've been skinned and hung from trees like sides of beef. As Schaefer leads his unit and a

captured guerilla named Anna (Elpidia Carrillo) back to civilization, something terrifying and inexplicable begins to happen. The men are killed, one by one, by an unknown, invisible predator (Kevin Peter Hall) from another world.

With the unit reversing roles— the hunters are now the hunted— the men (and woman) join forces against the enemy who blends into the jungle and manifests powers that far exceed any human's. It is ultimately up to Schaefer, who is insufficiently equipped to handle his opponent, to combine brains and brawn— not only to survive but to destroy the creature he has come to loathe.

Shot in the steamy Mexican jungle, *Predator* blends sci-fi, horror, and action. In order to convincingly push across that last ingredient Arnold and his co-

The macho cast of Predator made for an eclectic group of actors. From left to right: Shane Black, also a renowned screenwriter; Sonny Landham, often cast as a villain; a grim-looking Arnold; Carl Weathers, best known as Apollo Creed in Rocky; Bill Duke, also a film and TV director; and Jesse Ventura, a former professional wrestler.

stars attended a sort of "boot camp." Activities included running, climbing trees, rappeling down ropes, and intensive practice with weapon handling. After eight hours of camp every day, the actors went into rehearsal of their scenes.

Predator was slickly directed by John McTiernan, who would later helm *Die Hard* and *The Hunt for Red October*. Critical reaction to *Predator* was generally favorable; reviewers liked the breathtaking pace and nonstop action, although they didn't fail to mention implausibilities of the plot. For example, Roger Ebert wrote in the *Chicago Sun-Times*, "The action moves so quickly

that we overlook questions such as 1) Why would an alien species go to all the effort to send a creature to earth, just so that it could swing from trees and skin American soldiers? Or, 2) Why would a creature so technologically advanced need to bother with hand-to-hand combat, when it could just zap Arnold with a ray gun?"

But *Predator*, which was described by many moviegoers as a cross between *Rambo* and *Alien*, was considered absorbing enough to make such questions academic. High on the list of the film's strong points is the title creature, a special-effects triumph designed by Stan Winston. Humanoid but

Arnold, as Dutch Shaefer, confers with his men about the mysterious enemy that is cutting them down one by one. Elpidia Carrillo, the only woman with a significant role, plays a captured guerrilla fighter who knows more about the seemingly invisible alien than the men. The alien hunts the men for sport, or for his own pleasure, much like humans hunt various species for sport. The film can be taken as a comment on the pleasure humans find in violence, a point that comes across when the tables are turned and Dutch and his men are hunted down like animals. At the end, the Predator cynically snarls at Dutch,"I am what you are."

Above and right: Dutch is the leader of an elite military rescue team who travels the world secretly resolving potentially hot political situations. **Opposite:** Though Dutch has assembled a crack team of specialists, they are no match for the Predator.

sporting physical features that look alternately reptilian and crustacean, the Predator "sees" with intriguing infrared vision. This notion, expressed via clever polarization effects, allowed for interesting shots from the monster's point of view.

Carl Weathers, memorable as boxer Apollo Creed in the *Rocky* movies, brought his formidable physique and a sharp edge to his role as Dillon, while professional wrestler Jesse Ventura gave a lively performance as Blain.

With the script's emphasis on danger and flashy action sequences, *Predator* doesn't contain too much mirth. But, as *People* writer Ralph Novak noted, Arnold, who's "considerably slimmed down . . . manages to be likable even though there's little overt humor [because] he never seems to take things too seriously." Which means that, by this point in his career, the actor had developed a screen persona complex enough to compensate even for scripts that may not have been perfectly tailored to him.

In many ways, though, *Predator* is a typical Schwarzenegger vehicle, and one that satisfied his fans. It grossed a mammoth $70 million and marked a new turning point in the movie industry's perception of the Austrian muscleman. Arnold was evolving into a superstar.

And the star himself was pleased with his character and the final product. "I play a character

who is always in control of the situation," he said, "but all of a sudden, this unknown comes in, something I've never dealt with before in my life—then it becomes scary. And I become very vulnerable.

"I enjoyed playing a character who's part of a team," he continued, "a commander surrounded by men who are equally powerful, equally well trained. It's much more realistic to have a group of guys working together than to rely entirely on yourself."

Finally, Arnold is likely to recall *Predator* with special fondness, since it was during the film's shoot that he tied the knot with Maria Shriver.

THE RUNNING MAN
(1987)
Tri-Star Pictures
With
Arnold Schwarzenegger,
Maria Conchita Alonso,
Yaphet Kotto,
Jim Brown,
Jesse Ventura,
Mick Fleetwood,
Dweezil Zappa,
Marvin J. McIntire,
Richard Dawson.
Directed by Paul Michael Glaser.
Written by Steven E. DeSouza.
100 minutes.

Imagine a cross between *Rollerball*, *The Most Dangerous Game*, and the worst excesses of TV game shows. That's *The Running Man*, a big-budget action thriller that allowed Arnold to return to the science-fiction genre. He played Ben Richards, a policeman wrongly accused of murdering 1,500 innocent people in the totalitarian state that America has become in the year 2019. Ben is imprisoned but manages to escape with pals Laughlin (Yaphet Kotto) and Weiss (Marvin J. McIntire). The trio finds refuge with the underground resistance movement led by a father and son team (Mick Fleetwood and Dweezil Zappa). His friends join the movement, but Ben's only goal is to find his brother and escape the city. In his brother's apartment, he finds a new tenant, Amber Mendez (Maria Conchita Alonso), a jingle writer for the all-powerful state television network. Amber becomes an unwilling participant in Ben's escape effort.

Unfortunately, Ben is captured and, like other convicts, is forced to participate in a popular televised game show that makes sport out of the unarmed contestants' race against time— and against a select group of athletic, highly trained assassins. This fearsome group (Jim Brown, Toru Tanaka, Erland Van Lidth, and Gus Rethwisch) is called "the Stalkers." They're a well-armed bunch, equipped with flame throwers, electric saws, and razor-edged hockey sticks. Ben's race, then, is for nothing less than his survival.

The state-controlled media has turned Ben into a notorious, highly visible figure. His participation in the game show is

The Running Man brims with the look of futurist technology. Here, the character played by Arnold is at the mercy of that technology— but only temporarily.

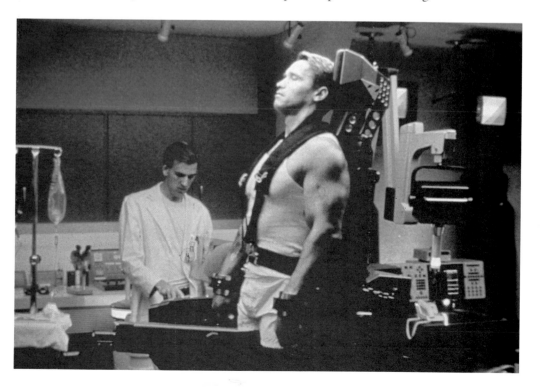

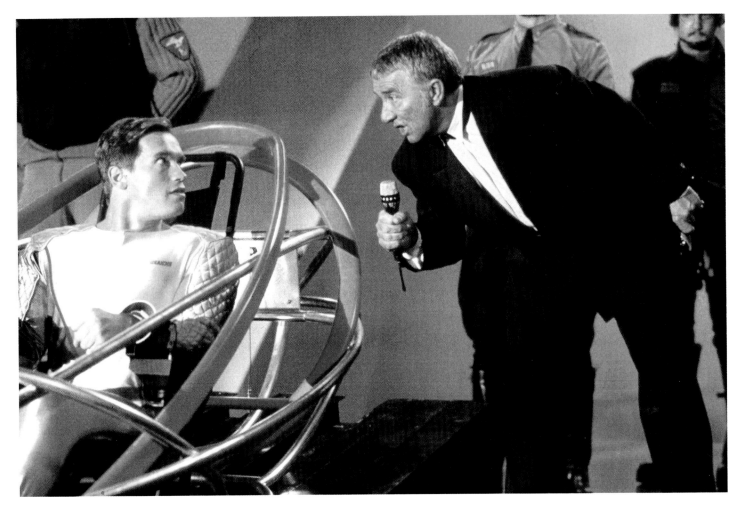

the idea of the show's ratings-crazed emcee, Damon Killian (Richard Dawson). Killian uses Ben's pals and Amber as bait for extra excitement. The game show's futuristic arena—actually a devastated section of L.A.—is where Ben gets to make mincemeat out of his pursuers, but not before he takes the audience on a rollercoaster ride of thrills and chills.

A special treat for action-film fans is the presence of former football great Jim Brown, cast as one of the colorfully costumed game-show assassins. Brown had hit movies in a big way in the mid-1960s and found success as star of "blaxploitation" pictures

of the early '70s. His career had sputtered in the intervening years, so audiences welcomed his lively role in *The Running Man*.

The Running Man, based on a novel by Stephen King writing under the nom de plume Richard Bachman, is a hard-edged, futuristic nightmare that won good reviews and respectable box office receipts—more than $30 million. Arnold was spared the critical sneers that had typified reaction to many of his earlier films. Adding to the picture's allure was the game-show format that the film adopts, thereby involving the audience in its nasty, exhilarating entertainment. Some critics noted that the film

Not all critics were pleased with The Running Man, but they were nearly unanimous in their praise for Family Feud's Richard Dawson (above right), who was cast as the unscrupulous game-show host.

"I try to put humor in <u>every</u> scene, and sometimes the director explains to me that it wouldn't work. And many times he's right."
A.S.

Arnold and co-star Maria Conchita Alonso made an appealing—and very physical—screen team.

could be perceived as a clever send-up of television and as a sharply cautionary tale about the medium's sinister potential for mind control. But other reviewers, like *People*'s Ralph Novak, wondered about "where the film stops lampooning TV audiences' thirst for vicarious violence and starts exploiting it."

Whether or not *The Running Man* is exploitative is debatable, but the casting of onetime *Family Feud* host Richard Dawson as Damon Killian certainly showed a sense of humor. Who better to play an ambitious, hyper-energetic TV star?

Although much praise was lavished on Dawson's witty line readings, Arnold got the biggest laughs. The script's humor is crude but effective, as when Ben uses a buzz saw to rip an antagonist in two, a violent act that causes him to quip, "He had

to split!" One-liners of this sort had already become a Schwarzenegger trademark, and audiences ate them up. Once again, Arnold had chosen a vehicle well; *The Running Man* was his best-received movie since *The Terminator*.

More importantly, the film solidified Schwarzenegger's status in Hollywood. The hefty $3 million salary he received for the picture couldn't go anywhere but up, and he showed that he could hold his own with talented actors the caliber of Yaphet Kotto and Maria Conchita Alonso. But even in terms of image, *The Running Man* is significant because it left no doubt as to Arnold's ability to play the underdog—the guy who turns the tables on his oppressors. The approach worked beautifully here, and opened up new avenues for Arnold to explore as a screen star.

"I don't mind doing a scene over and over again. It's not really patience. Each time I do it, I see myself getting better and better—going toward perfection."
A.S.

Above left: Few actors are as respected in Hollywood for their ability as Yaphet Kotto (right). It's a tribute to Arnold's own talents as an actor that he gave up nothing in his scenes with Kotto. **Left:** Arnold faces off against actor Gus Rethwisch, cast as one of the "Stalkers" who pursues Ben Richards, the Running Man.

RED HEAT
(1988)
Tri-Star Pictures
With
Arnold Schwarzenegger,
James Belushi,
Peter Boyle,
Ed O'Ross,
Larry Fishburne,
Gina Gershon,
Richard Bright.
Directed by Walter Hill.
Written by Harry Kleiner & Walter Hill
and Troy Kennedy Martin.
106 minutes.

Red Heat pits two very different men against each other: Captain Ivan Danko (Arnold), the taciturn, relentless Russian homicide cop known in Moscow as "Iron Jaw," and Detective Sergeant Art Ridzik (James Belushi), a wisecracking Chicago plainclothesman, known for his lax attitude and penchant for cutting corners. These cultural and temperamental polar opposites are forced into an alliance when the Russian comes to the Windy City to track down a notorious, murderous Russian drug dealer named Viktor Rostavili (Ed O'Ross), who's just

This page: Actor Jim Belushi built a successful film career on comic roles, often as a wisecracking guy with a cynical sense of humor. His pairing with the strong-but-silent Arnold was a clever idea.

been arrested locally on a minor traffic violation.

Much of the pleasure of *Red Heat* comes from the contrast between the characters of Ridzik and Danko. While the reluctant plainclothes cop annoys Danko by shooting off his mouth about anything—including the drawbacks of his new partner's

social and political systems—the Russian remains focused on his goal. The relationship evolves when Danko loses custody of Viktor in an ambush by the mobster's gang. A Chicago cop is killed in the process, which inspires Ridzik to become a real partner to the Russian. The two embark on a relentless search for the fugitive, freely disregarding police procedure and alienating Commander Donnelly (Peter Boyle). The pair delve into the Chicago underworld and, in the process, get to know each other and establish a curious sort of rapport. Along the way, much of Chicago is destroyed before Viktor is brought to heel.

Red Heat was director Walter Hill's attempt to duplicate the success of his own *48 Hours*, another unrestrained action film that featured mismatched partners who must work together toward a common goal. Hill asked Arnold to lose 10 pounds ("so I would look more Slavic," as the star told *US* magazine) and study Russian. Further realism

came from a number of scenes that were shot on location in Moscow's Red Square. The result was that *Red Heat* turned out to be a moderate box-office hit.

Reviewers noted the picture's slickness and technical adeptness, but remained cool to the film, lamenting its use of stereotypes and routine odd-couple comic shticks. Still, Schwarzenegger's charm hardly eluded them. As Richard Corliss wrote in *Time*, "Arnold, starched tongue in cheek, is a doll: G.I. Joe in Soviet mufti. He could beat the stuffing out of a toy Rambo."

Arnold was ideally cast as the imposing Soviet cop of Red Heat. Whether displaying his awesome physique (above) or merely looking stern in uniform (left), Ivan Danko seems a character to be reckoned with.

TWINS
(1988)
Universal
With
Arnold Schwarzenegger,
Danny DeVito,
Kelly Preston,
Chloe Webb,
Bonnie Bartlett,
Marshall Bell,
Trey Wilson.
Directed by Ivan Reitman.
Written by William Davies & William
Osborne and Timothy Harris & Hershel
Weingrod.
115 minutes.

Above and right: A clever ad campaign prepared audiences to howl with laughter at the absurdity of Arnold Schwarzenegger and Danny DeVito's casting as twins. Romantic interludes, and even simple scenes that revolve around wardrobe choices, were funny enough to keep box offices humming.

Twins is the story of identical siblings Julius (Arnold) and Vincent Benedict (Danny DeVito). They are the offspring of a botched government genetics experiment, and have been separated since birth. Funny things happen when the brothers are reunited at age 35. Julius is the perfect specimen of a man in body and soul, but he's also inexperienced. This innocent man-child, raised in a controlled environment on a tropical island, travels to Los Angeles to search for his brother, Vincent, who's a diminutive, obnoxious, small-time thief with neither brains nor brawn. Julius locates Vincent in jail. While the "perfect" brother is devoted to the notion of family loyalty, Vincent regards his twin merely as a dopey bodyguard.

After being joined by sexy sisters Linda (Chloe Webb) and Marnie (Kelly Preston), Julius and Victor hit the road. Julius hopes to locate their long-lost mother, while Vincent is eager to snag a big payoff from his latest scam. During the course of their adventure, the twins learn a valuable lesson about the importance of being brothers. Julius helps steer Victor straight, while he himself learns to drink beer, romance Marnie, and use a microwave.

Twins is based on one of those irresistibly contrived premises that moviemakers like to call "high concept." Briskly directed by Ivan Reitman, the director of *Ghostbusters*, the film was

promoted via a highly effective publicity campaign that pictured the two mismatched stars dressed identically and exuding the same jubilant bravado. The campaign's tag line was "Only their mother can tell them apart."

Although some critics saw *Twins* as a silly, one-joke effort, others were amused. Audiences certainly had a great time, pushing the picture's gross to a whopping $110 million, more than that of any of Schwarzenegger's previous films. The magnitude of this box-office success propelled his career into the stratosphere.

With this, his first overt foray into comedy, Arnold won new fans and became a superstar. David Ansen of *Newsweek* wrote, "He's endearingly, incongruously sweet. For the first time since *Stay Hungry* he's a recognizable

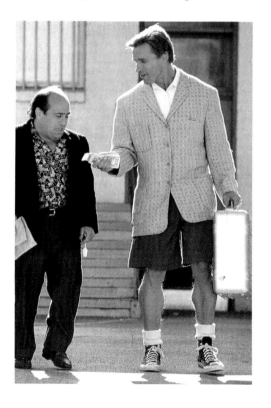

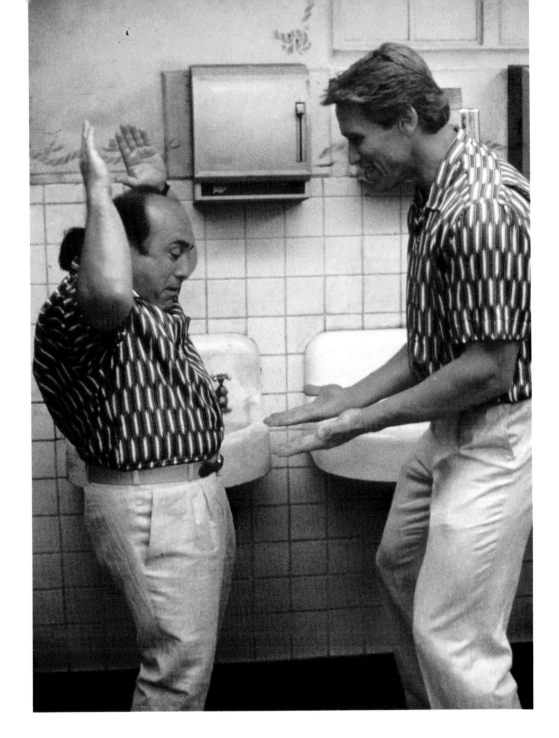

"In my last five or six movies, my love relationship was basically with guns, with explosives, with grenades and missiles. [Twins] was for me a learning experience all the way through."
A.S.; <u>Marquee</u>

Above: The naive Julius (Arnold) locates brother Vincent (DeVito) in jail. **Above left:** Undeterred, he becomes Vincent's friend and learns how to loosen up.

member of our species." Similarly, Bob Strauss of *Movieline* praised Arnold's comic timing, adding, "he captures the character's built-in naiveté and never makes him seem stupid. Hard stuff." Almost every other critic noted the easy, goofy chemistry between the two stars, and the way in which the pair's comic scenes clicked. The wacky casting had paid off.

Arnold remarked, "I've learned some mechanical things from Danny, because he's done comedy for so long. It's been a very good learning experience. It was very exciting for me, because I'm finally getting into the kind of movies I've always wanted to be in—movies that are not all muscle."

TOTAL RECALL
(1990)
Tri-Star Pictures
With
Arnold Schwarzenegger,
Rachel Ticotin,
Sharon Stone,
Ronny Cox,
Michael Ironside,
Marshall Bell,
Mel Johnson, Jr.
Directed by Paul Verhoeven.
Written by Ronald Shusett & Dan
O'Bannon and Gary Goldman.
109 minutes.

Total Recall is set in the year 2084, in a society ruled by two opposing government factions. Mars, which has already been colonized, suffers political unrest. A construction worker on Earth, Doug Quaid (Arnold), is haunted in his dreams by real-seeming memories of a past life on Mars—yet to his knowledge he has never been to the planet. The dreams intensify and Quaid's grasp of reality begins to crumble; the line between the real and the unreal becomes increasingly blurred, until Quaid realizes that everything he thinks he knows and has experienced may well be a fabrication. His mental state worries his beautiful wife, Lori (Sharon Stone), and deteriorates further when he visits Rekall, Inc., a travel service specializing in implanting artificial "memories" of fantasy adventures in the minds of its customers. Obsessed with Mars, Quaid signs up for a fabricated adventure on the planet but the procedure goes haywire. In the process, a separate, long-suppressed facet of Quaid's personality comes to the fore.

Quaid quickly realizes that his dreams have a basis in truth. He also discovers that he is under surveillance, and that the people who are following him are worried about what he may remember. They want him dead, so Quaid flees to Mars. There, he antagonizes Cohaagen (Ronny Cox), the colony's ruthless dictator, and meets a beautiful guerilla fighter named Melina (Rachel Ticotin). Quaid learns that his loving wife Lori isn't his wife at all, but a deadly agent; his memories of their courtship and wedding day have been artificially implanted in his brain. Even more intriguing is Quaid's

Right: Total Recall is a masterpiece of special effects and set design; an entire Martian city was created for this fast-paced sci-fi thriller. **Opposite:** Arnold holds the fantastic disguise that assumes a life of its own. The head was designed by makeup technician Rob Bottin.

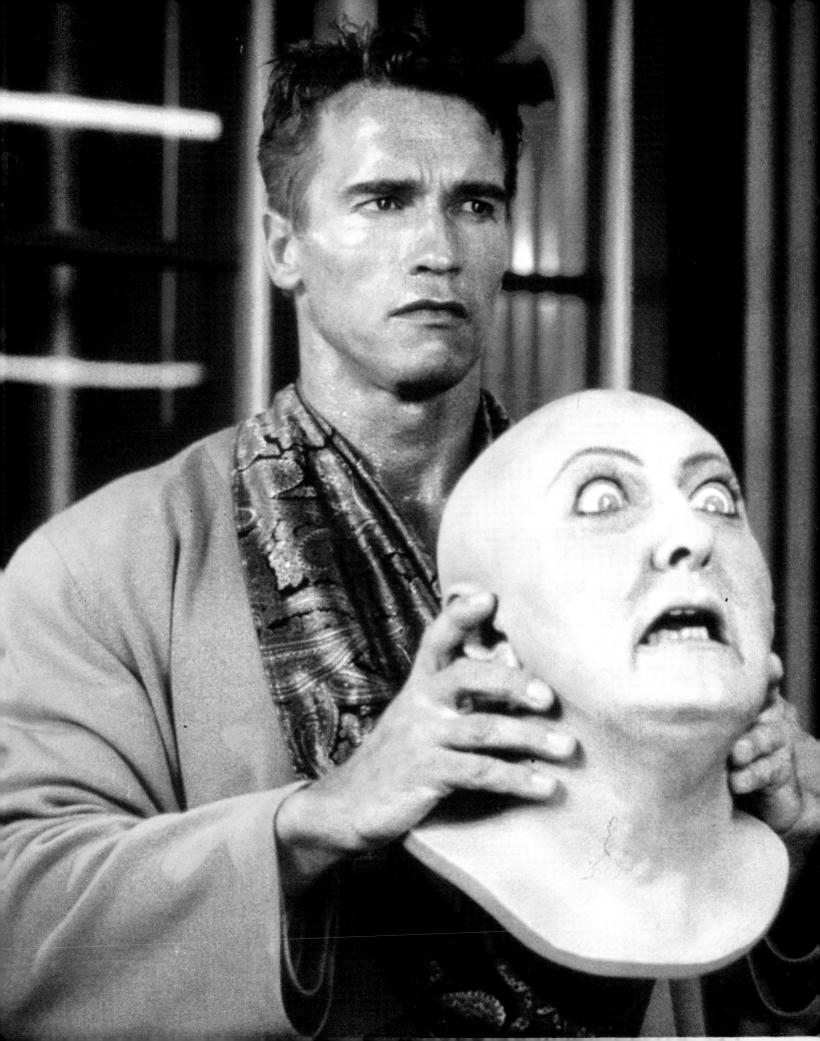

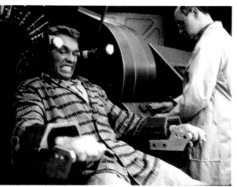

Top: Arnold meets Total Recall's animatronic cabdriver. **Above:** The beginning of a very bad experience at Rekall, Inc. **Right:** The star with director Paul Verhoeven.

discovery that, under the name Hauser, he was once a spy in the employ of Cohaagen. Now, the dictator sees Quaid as a dangerous liability, and enlists the fanatical intelligence agent Richter (Michael Ironside) to eliminate him.

A wisecracking black cab driver (Mel Johnson, Jr.) pretends to be of service to Quaid, but turns out to be a mutant who follows his passenger to the hiding place of George (Marshall Bell), the enigmatic rebel commander, who's also a mutant. Although the rebel hideout is destroyed by Cohaagen's men, Quaid and Melina get the last laugh when they propel Cohaagen into the nearly airless void outside the colony, and destroy the nuclear reactor that limits the colony's supply of oxygen. The once miserable inhabitants of Mars can finally—and literally—breathe freely.

Total Recall was based on a short story by noted science-fiction writer Phillip K. Dick. The film was far and away Arnold's most provocative and complex to date. Budgeted at $50 million (some sources quoted even higher figures), the picture opened to smash box office numbers and good reviews. Critics and general audiences responded positively to the film's exhilarating mix of sci-fi, violent action, dazzling special effects, and the haunting psychological mystery that is at the core of the story.

Directed by Paul Verhoeven, a Dutch director best known for *Robocop*, the picture manifested layers of meaning beyond the slam-bang entertainment that Arnold was expected to deliver. The star himself was paid $11 million for his participation, plus 15 percent of the profits, an enormous salary by any standard. Yet when the box-office gross of *Total Recall* passed the $110 million mark, Schwarzenegger proved to be worth every penny.

According to Verhoeven, quoted in *Movies USA, Total Recall* "is about identity—it's a Kafkaesque nightmare about a mind being stolen. That's a modern psychosis." Arnold agrees. "It's a wild mind trip," he told *Movies USA*. He felt he was taking part in a unique enterprise. "When I first read the script," he remarked to *Starlog,* "during the days when I was doing *Commando,* it just stayed with me . . . I could not put it down.

"This is something people have not seen me in," the actor continued. "It's not a leap in the other direction the way *Twins* was," he conceded, but it offered a challenge in terms of the ambitious subject matter, as well as the chance to do what amounted to a dual role.

"It is a challenge," Schwarzenegger stressed in the *Starlog* interview, "because you're not coming in with the same character that you're going out with. Hauser's an interesting character, but Quaid's just this big program. . . ."

In the movie, Arnold has a pretty elaborate love scene with Sharon Stone, who takes the part of the agent who masquerades as Quaid's loving wife. By this point in his career, the actor had developed a technique as to how to deal with such potentially

Arnold and actress Sharon Stone steamed up the screen in this torrid love scene from Total Recall.

"It's easy to put the action together. I know how to do that."
A.S.

The budget of Total Recall was enormous, much of it going for elaborate sets and props like the ones seen here.

awkward scenes. He told *Movies USA*, "I talk to the girl; you talk about being half-naked in bed. You get the inhibitions out of the way in rehearsal."

Arnold did not shy away from the moment in *Total Recall* when Quaid does away with his "wife." Caught suddenly in a kill-or-be-killed situation, Quaid shoots Lori dead. It's a grim moment that's lightened somewhat by a bit of Schwarzenegger-style humor. "But I'm your wife," Lori pleads. Quaid pulls the trigger, then regards the corpse. "Consider that a divorce," he says.

"Humor during scenes of violence," Verhoeven told *USA Today*, "takes the reality away a bit and protects the audience. Arnie's line before or after these scenes brings the realism to a different level. Without the humor, it may be too strong."

On the set, in Churubusco Studios in Mexico City, Arnold injected a similar cheerfulness. "He comes on the set and everyone is happier," Rachel Ticotin told *Marquee*. "I see it as a responsibility," Arnold admitted to the same magazine. "But I don't make any effort. I'm a naturally happy guy."

Still, *Total Recall* is rough, tough entertainment. It's interesting to note that Verhoeven and the special effects crew actually made an effort to see that the film wasn't *too* intense. For instance, the mutants who populate Mars are startling in appearance, but not so

"When you're alone and you stick your neck out for a particular cause, that's heroic. A lot of people want to do that in real life, which is why my movies are such a great escape."
A.S.

grotesque as to shock the audience. Similarly, care was taken to see that the nightmarish quality of the story and the film's vision of the future were not excessively depressing and dark. The filmmakers wanted to disturb a little and entertain a lot. They succeeded on both counts, and in grand style.

Top: Rachel Ticotin is lively and appealing as the fearless woman who wins the hero's heart. **Above:** Ronny Cox played Cohaagen, the viciously unprincipled dictator of Mars.

KINDERGARTEN COP
(1990)
Universal
With
Arnold Schwarzenegger,
Penelope Ann Miller,
Pamela Reed,
Linda Hunt,
Richard Tyson,
Carroll Baker.
Directed by Ivan Reitman.
Written by Murray Salem and Herschel
Weingrod & Timothy Harris.
110 minutes.

Above: The smash comedy <u>Kindergarten Cop</u> gave Arnold, pictured here with Penelope Ann Miller, another opportunity to display his skill as a romantic leading man. **Right and opposite top:** The picture also let Arnold get physical, but in a cheerful, silly way.

Detective John Kimble (Arnold) must forget everything he knows about the mean streets of Los Angeles and prepare for a mission of a different kind altogether: In order to catch a murderous drug dealer who has been ripped off by his ex-wife, Kimble must go undercover as a kindergarten teacher. That's the premise of *Kindergarten Cop,* Schwarzenegger's most recent comic success.

The villain is Cullen Crisp (Richard Tyson), who is searching not only for his money, but for the son he hasn't seen for five years. To entrap him, Kimble—assisted by his partner and pal, Phoebe O'Hara (Pamela Reed)—has to function convincingly in a job for which he is, to say the least, ill suited. The diminutive school principal,

Mrs. Schlowski (Linda Hunt), senses there's something wrong about the new teacher and stands watchfully over him, while teacher Joyce Paulmarie (Penelope Ann Miller), who has a son in Kimble's class, becomes both his love interest and a suspect in Kimble's case. The cop also has to face other less-than-friendly characters, such as Eleanor Crisp (Carroll Baker), the gun-totin' grandmother of the drug dealer's son. Ultimately, though, it's Kimble's relationship with a bunch of rambunctious five-year-olds that gives *Kindergarten Cop* its charm.

The picture reunited Arnold with the director and some of the writers of *Twins.* It won gentle reviews and went on to gross an impressive $85 million, firmly establishing the actor as a comic

Left: Much of the film's humor lies in the fact that the cop—confident and intimidating in his own world—finds himself completely at the mercy of his young charges. He can bluster all he wants, but the kids know they have the upper hand.

draw. The movie called upon him to reveal his lighter, more vulnerable side; to see him struggle with his tough guy persona in that context was delightful. The role also eased Arnold into a screen romance with more confidence than ever before. His success here as a "leading man" will undoubtedly pave the way for more mainstream roles. As Roger Ebert wrote in *The Chicago Sun-Times,*

that involve children. The actor himself estimated the picture could have grossed another $25 million if it had toned down such scenes. In all, though, he feels that the criticisms in this regard are "totally unjustified," as he told *Interview.* "We made a really conscious effort not to be violent. But what made the film different was that it told the story of this tough cop who's thrown into this situation where none of his tough tactics work. Through that you got into comedy. . . ."

. Acting alongside children wasn't a problem for Arnold, himself a recent father. "I felt comfortable about not being upstaged," he told the *Manhattan*

Above: On the city's mean streets, Arnold is in complete command.
Right: Dealing with a gaggle of five-year-olds is something else altogether!

"When [Schwarzenegger] plays a love scene . . . he is touchingly sincere. He uses gentleness, not machismo; he behaves toward a woman as a protector, not an aggressor. John Wayne often used the same approach."

But the movie, which also deals with the subjects of child abuse, drugs, and divorce, did trigger some mild controversy by virtue of including violent scenes

"[Director] Ivan Reitman's strength is that he can look at situations that could be very serious and then make them very funny. That's why he's the number one comedy director."
A.S.; <u>Kindergarten Cop</u> press kit

Spirit. "But, more importantly, I don't care about being upstaged . . . . I am hard to hide in a movie. . . ." he laughed. He confided to a studio-publicity interviewer that he found acting with children "almost like doing a movie with special effects. You always get surprised, you don't know what is going to happen next and nothing happens the same way twice. I was always caught off guard, so I had to be quick to improvise.

"The character I play in this movie goes through a complete transformation," he continued. "At first, he's a cop who knows only one thing—his job. And the way he goes about it sometimes rubs even the police department the wrong way. And then all of a sudden he goes undercover and has the painful experience of facing 30 children in the classroom with absolutely no idea how to communicate with them. It changes him completely."

The success of *Kindergarten Cop* brought Arnold closer to his stated goal: less muscle, more laughter. And greater stardom.

Top: A teacher's work is never done. **Above:** Thank goodness for the sweet relief of romance.

57

TERMINATOR 2: JUDGMENT DAY
(1991)
Tri-Star Pictures
With
Arnold Schwarzenegger,
Linda Hamilton,
Edward Furlong,
Robert Patrick,
Joe Morton.
Directed by James Cameron.
Written by James Cameron & William
Wisher.
135 minutes.

In *Terminator 2: Judgment Day* a new, more deadly Terminator (Robert Patrick) goes back in time to try again to prevent mankind from triumphing over the ruling machines in a future war. Sarah Connor (Linda Hamilton) is the mother of John (Edward Furlong), her 10-year-old son by Kyle Reese (played by Michael Biehn in the original movie). Although just a child now, John is destined to grow up to become the leader of the anti-machine resistance, and prevent the nuclear holocaust of 1997—the Judgment Day of the film's title. So it is that the future-era machines have declared that John must die.

To protect the boy, the human resistance sends another Terminator (Arnold) from the future—a cyborg programmed to be as relentless in his defense of the boy as his nemesis is bent on the child's destruction. ·

After alerting the boy to the danger he's in, the cyborg allies himself with the child to free Sarah from the mental institution where she's been held because of her apocalyptic prophecies. The three must now face the more advanced new model T-1000 Terminator, who, unlike the previous skin-covered model, is a molten-metal cyborg capable of assuming and abandoning human form at will. (In one horrifying moment, the T-1000 rises out of a checkerboard-tiled floor and seamlessly oozes into a cop without skipping a beat.)

While the "old model" Terminator starts out as a killing machine, inhuman and unthinking, he becomes gradually humanized by his young protégé, who makes him promise never to shoot to kill again.

Sarah decides that the only way to alter the future is to change the present, so she plans

Right: Terminator 2 is a relentlessly exciting game of search-and-destroy. Here, Arnold, Linda Hamilton, and Edward Furlong hope they've eluded the T-1000. **Opposite:** Despite his futuristic origins, the Terminator has a fondness for 20th century weaponry, such as this fearsome assault rifle.

Arnold and Edward Furlong had a special chemistry together that made the few non-action scenes believable. Here, the old-model Terminator 101 and young John Connor escape the pursuit of the T-1000.

enormous explosions, and a final, deadly confrontation in a steel mill.

Coming in at a budget of some $94 million, *Terminator 2* is the most expensive film ever made. It's also one of the most spectacular action/sci-fi thrillers ever produced. Unlike the modest conception of the original *Terminator*, there is nothing modest about this sequel, which grossed a phenomenal $70 million in its opening week and may well become one of the biggest-grossing pictures of all time.

Unlike most other mega-budget movies, where their very cost arouses hostility among critics for the sheer waste involved, *Terminator 2* aroused no such reaction. The reason: All of the money that was spent can be seen on the screen. Chief among these visible attributes is Arnold himself, who received an $11 million jet as payment for his performance. The movie officially confirms Schwarzenegger's status as the world's most popular movie star. It is the absolute peak of his career, surpassing even *Total Recall* as the Austrian muscleman's ultimate vehicle. And this time he has a lot more dialogue than the 17 lines he had in the original *Terminator*, a measure of his growing confidence as an actor.

"I've been offered a lot of money to do sequels to my other films, like *Predator* and *Commando*," Arnold told *US* magazine, "but the only one I really wanted to do was

to kill Miles Dyson (Joe Morton), the future creator of the T-1000. But the three manage to convince Dyson to destroy his own preliminary research that would in time have led to the creation of the T-1000. Undeterred, the T-1000 pursues the old-model Terminator and the humans, involving them in a wild variety of car-and-truck chases,

Terminator. I also made it clear I wouldn't do it without Jim."

Schwarzenegger was referring to director Jim Cameron, who had helmed the first *Terminator* adventure, and who went on to do *Aliens* and *The Abyss.* The star's decision to stick with Cameron was a wise one, for, as David Ansen noted in *Newsweek,* "Nobody knows how to use Schwarzenegger better than Cameron. He was born to play a machine. . . . As an emotion-less cyborg acting out the part of a foster father, he's impressive, hilarious, almost touching."

Terminator 2, which was shot in L.A. and other California locations, allows Arnold to repeat his most popular line from the original, "I'll be back!," and lets him coin a couple more, such as "Trust me!" and

"Hasta la vista, baby!" He is taught the latter phrase by John, in an especially funny scene in which the boy decides to make his cyborg protector "cool."

Arnold remarked to TV's David Letterman that the film allowed him to play "a kinder, gentler Terminator." He elaborated on the point during a chat with *Interview*: "There are certain feelings that I begin to understand by observing human beings. There is a wonderful scene where the boy cries and I say, 'What's wrong with your eyes?' Later I tell him that I have come to understand about crying, though it is something I could never do."

Initially, Cameron and Arnold kicked around the idea of casting Arnold as *both* Terminators, who would look alike despite their

"[Jim Cameron] has the same fanaticism for physical and visual detail [as on the first Terminator film]. But now he'll do a shot ten times over for the acting. Before he would be doing it eight times over for the look."

A.S.; Entertainment Weekly

Linda Hamilton, director James Cameron, Joe Morton, and Arnold confer about an important sequence in which Morton, as Miles Dyson, helps Sarah Connor and the old-model Terminator destroy the Cyberdyne Systems lab. Originally, the building explosion was planned to be filmed as a miniature effect during post-production, but Cameron insisted on staging it as a full-scale explosion.

inherent differences. The notion was nixed in favor of what Schwarzenegger told *Interview* would be a "more streamlined-looking character," the star's opposite.

Although Robert Patrick's physical elasticity (courtesy of computer graphics images by George Lucas's Industrial Light & Magic) is a show stopper, Arnold—attired in biker leather—is not easily eclipsed. Indeed, thanks to makeup wizard Stan Winston, he himself undergoes a remarkable physical transformation in the course of the adventure. "In the final stage," he told *Interview*, "my body is shot up. The chest is open, and you can see the steel coming through. The mechanism of the knee is exposed, and the flesh is hanging out. Half the flesh of the face is gone. Needless to say, I'm a big mess. . . ."

The appearance of Arnold's combat-abused face was a vital part of Terminator 2. As makeup designer Winston explained, "We were able to take what we did the first time and do it better the second time. A number of stages were designed as Arnold's Terminator deteriorates. An actor must know going into a situation like this that there is physical stress involved with this makeup process. Fortuantely for us, Arnold Schwarzenegger was a real pro throughout."

Winston, assisted by makeup artists Jefferson Dawn and Steve LaPorte, and by hair stylist Peter Tothpal, transformed Arnold into the Terminator some 35 times during the course of the shoot. The star's patience was undoubtedly put to the test, for the time needed for that many makeup sessions is equal to six days!

Enduring the application of makeup and waiting for complex special-effects shots to be set up were only part of the challenge faced by Arnold during the shoot; the real test came when the cameras began to roll. As Arnold told *T2 Movie Magazine*, "I had to act like a cyborg, which meant I couldn't show any kind of human fear or reaction to the fire, explosions, or gunfire that were going off around me. That can be difficult when you're walking through a door with its frame on fire, trying to reload a gun, and at the same time, thinking in the back of your mind that people have accidents doing these kinds of stunts and that it might be my turn." But Schwarzenegger added, "Every time you work in front of a camera with new actors and directors, it's a new growth experience. The more experience I've gained, the more confident I've become in my abilities as an actor."

Jim Cameron noted that Arnold appeared in only about 20 percent of the original *Terminator*, but is in nearly every scene of the sequel. Linda Hamilton underwent her own metamorphosis. Cast in the first film as a lonely, almost passive woman, she emerges in

Above: Though die-hard fans of the original film expressed some disappointment that Arnold was no longer the evil Terminator, he still cast a powerful image in the action scenes and performed some of his own stunts. **Opposite:** Arnold's costume is reminiscent of his threads in the original film, only more sleek and stylish.

Terminator 2 as a take-charge warrior who exhibits a bodybuilder's physique and a will of iron. "In her own way," Cameron told *Starlog*, "she has become a terminator herself."

While some critics were concerned about the film's extreme violence—*Entertainment Weekly*'s Owen Gleiberman termed it "a great big feast of wreckage"—the general reception was overwhelmingly positive. Reviewers applauded the film's exhilarating execution, and noted

Arnold and Maria proved irresistible to the media at the splashy premiere of Terminator 2.

the interesting paradox of the script's anti-violence message being presented via wall-to-wall brutality.

But the director doesn't see any contradiction here. "Our violent and aggressive nature is probably responsible for our success on this planet, equally

with our intelligence," he explained to a studio-publicity interviewer. "But the price that we have to pay is that we always hover on the edge of annihilation. Ultimately, the film is about the value of human life. This film empowers the individual. It says that no matter how inconsequential you may seem to others or even to yourself, your individual existence may have great value in the future."

Cameron continued, "*The Terminator* was a cultural phenomenon that people responded to on a psychological level. The Terminator represented the dark side of the human psyche, and audiences embraced the fantasy of being totally stripped of all moral constraints and having the ability to do exactly what they wanted whenever they wanted. It's a dark fantasy, but is one that people can have fun with. . . . "

Fun—and heavy doses of excitement—are what *Terminator 2* is all about. And those qualities sum up the screen appeal of Schwarzenegger. Caryn James of *The New York Times* went a step further, evaluating Arnold's role in *Terminator 2* and describing him as "the perfect Bush-era Terminator, a machine as sensitive war-hero." By contrast, she wrote, "The bad old Terminator [in the original movie] reflected the heady Reagan '80s. . . . As pop icons do, [Arnold] captures the temper of his times."